Dad's Bike

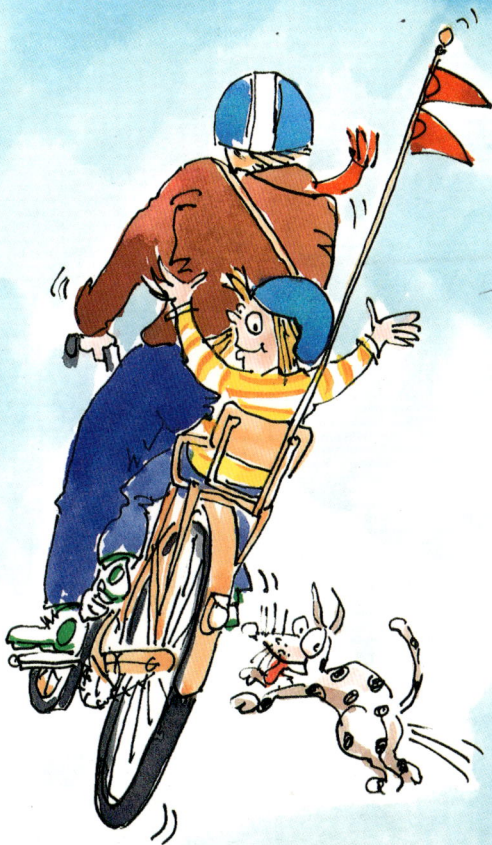

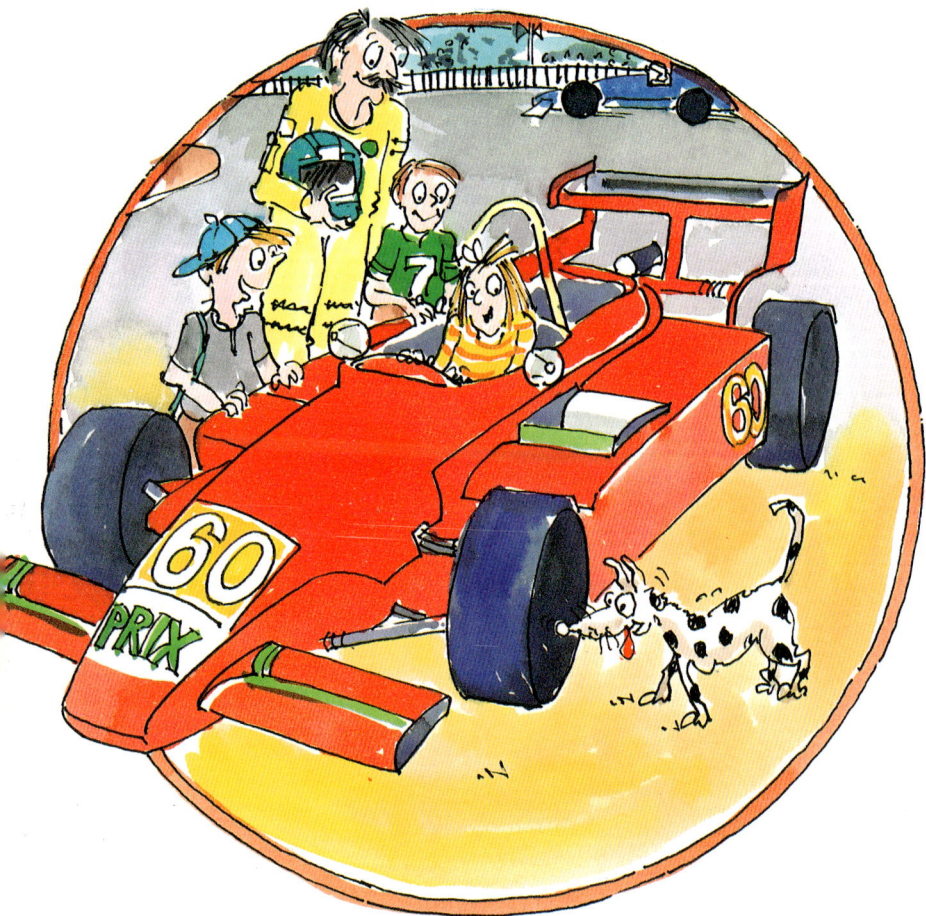

I wish I had a racing car

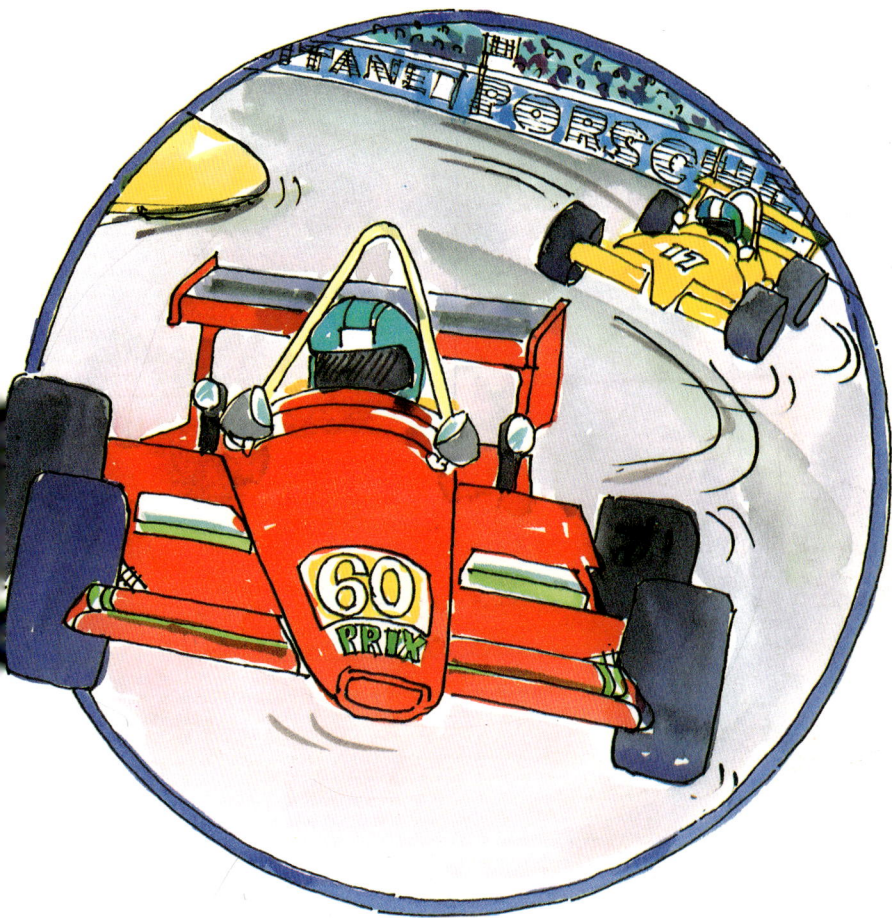

to race around the track.

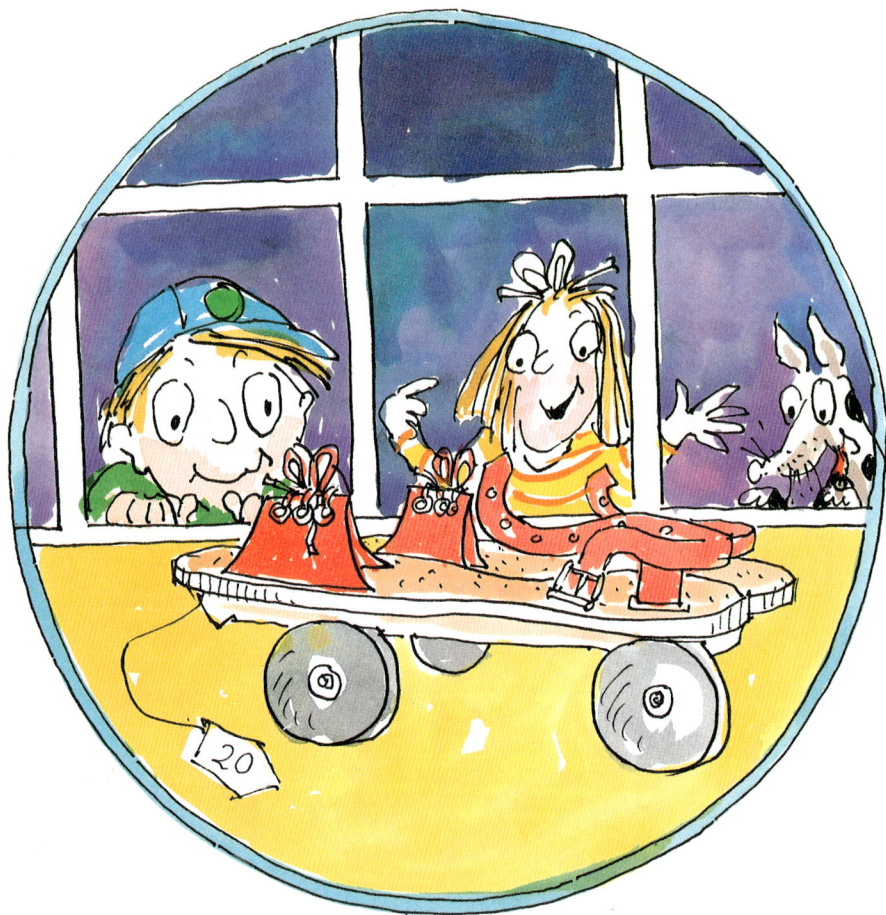

I wish I had some roller skates

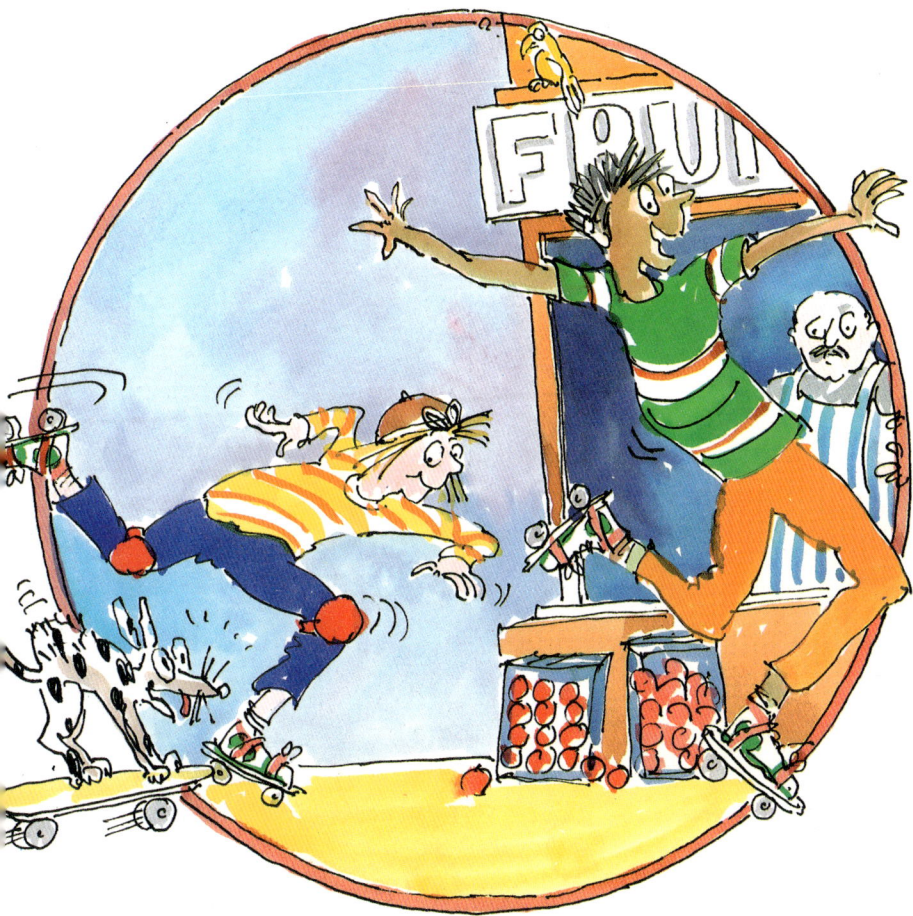

to skate to the store and back.

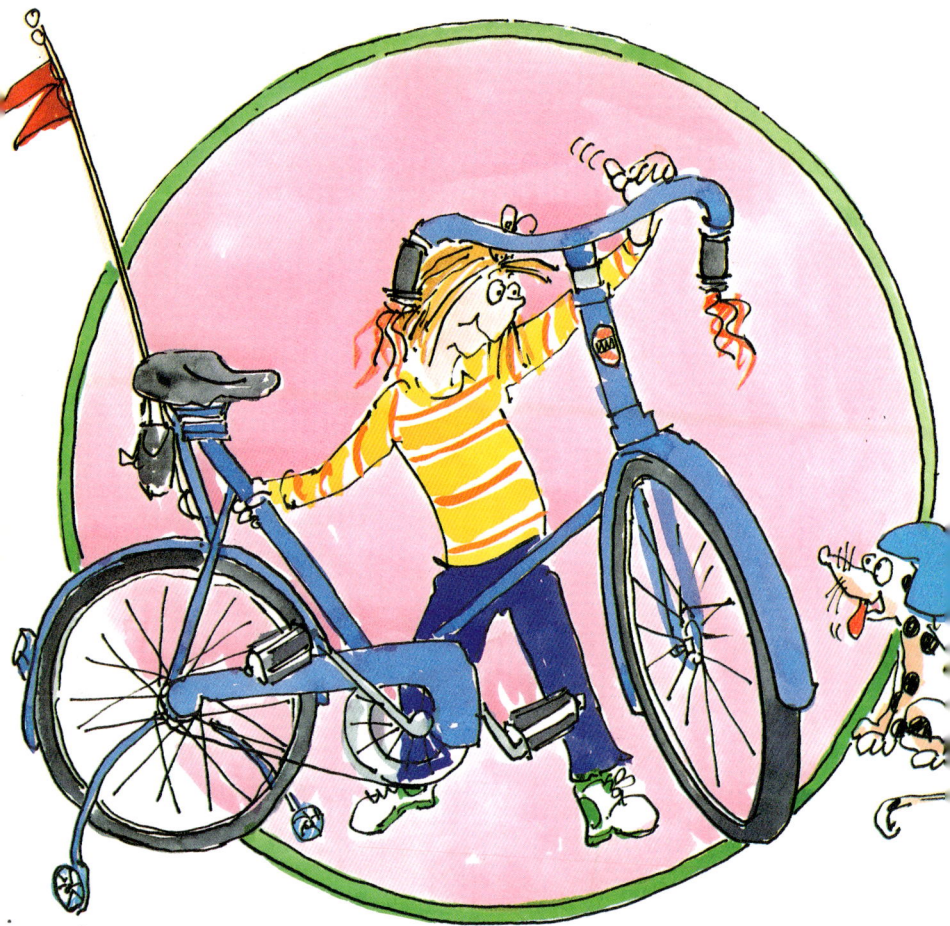

I wish I had a brand new bike.

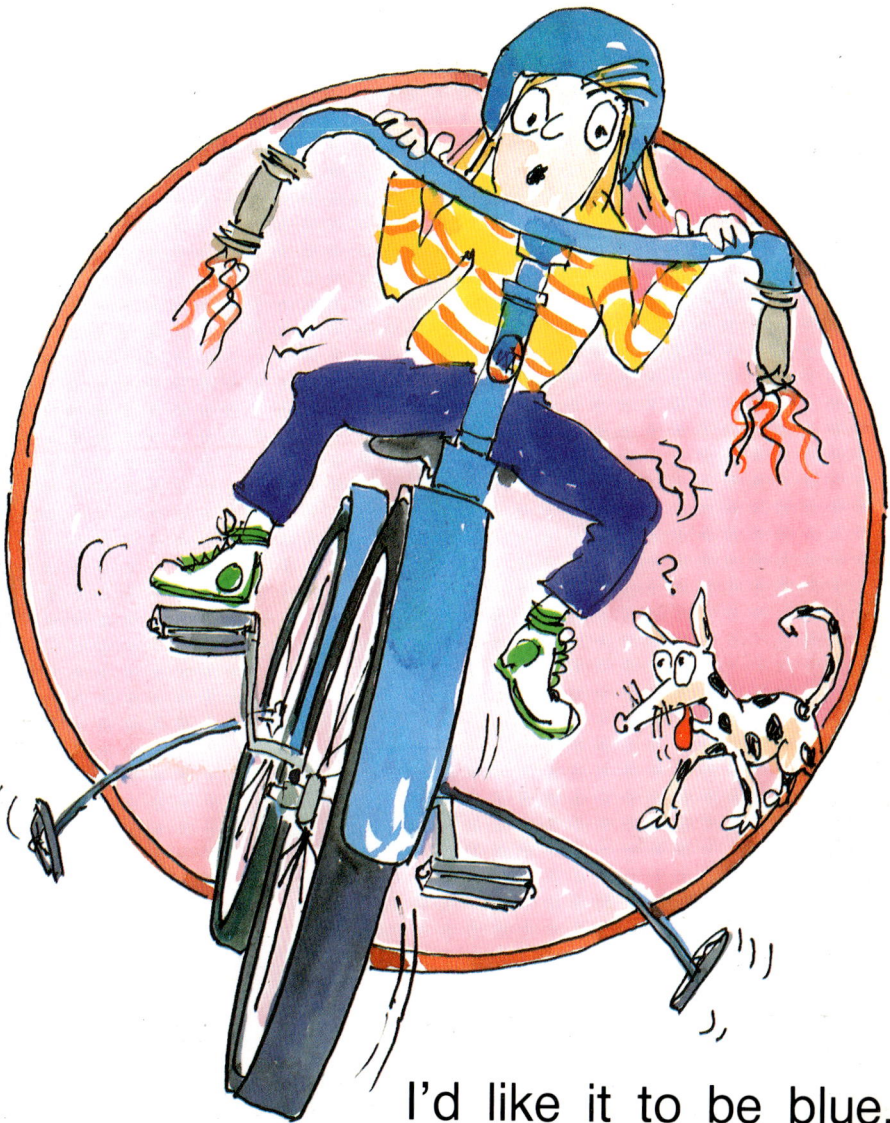

I'd like it to be blue.

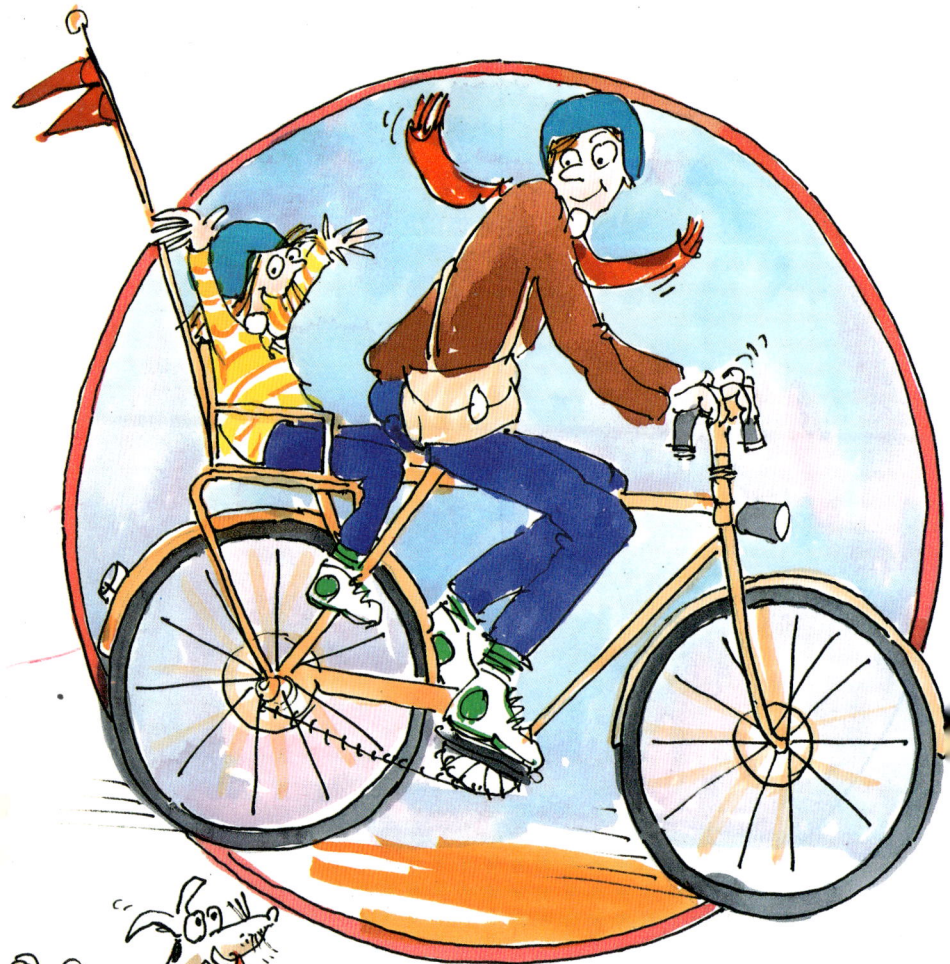

But until I'm big enough,
I guess Dad's bike will do.